*This book is dedicated to the memory
of my maternal grandmother,
Dora S. Lampson.*

Acknowledgments

The following poems, sometimes in a slightly different form, appeared in the following publications: 'West' and 'Amber' in *The Café Review*; 'Lips' in *The Irish Times*; 'Dust' in *Cyphers*; 'Barter' in *The Massachusetts Review*; 'Portal' in *The Moth Magazine*; and 'Trinity', 'Virago', 'Midges', 'Trying', and 'Judgment' in *The Common*.

Contents

Preface

The following long poem is based loosely on the letters of Abelard and Heloise as translated from the Latin by C. K. Scott Moncrieff. Published in 1925, his book is dedicated to George Moore, who himself wrote a novel about the fabled, medieval lovers and contributed his own epistolary forward to Moncrieff's handsome folio. Harriet O'Donovan Sheehy gave this book to me long ago, a gift from the library of Frank O'Connor, her deceased, first husband.

Pierre Abelard was a twelfth-century philosopher and theologian originally from Brittany. As a young philosophy student in Paris at the Cathedral School of Notre Dame, he famously defeated his teacher by presenting a superior exegesis of 'Ezekiel'. Abelard instantly became a celebrity. Subsequently, he took up lodging in the household of the uncle of a scholarly young woman named Heloise. Abelard tutored her and also made her pregnant. Heloise went to Brittany for her confinement with Abelard's family. She gave birth to a son, Astrolabe, the boy's name a tribute to his father's rational mind.

Both to protect his career as a celibate scholar and maintain moral rectitude, Abelard proposed a secret marriage to Heloise. She at first vigorously resisted this expeditious solution. Eventually she relented. When her uncle, however, publically disclosed the marriage, Abelard sent Heloise, who'd denied her uncle's claim, to a convent to be cared for by nuns. Her uncle, suspecting an evasion of responsibility on Abelard's part, arranged for his henchman to castrate the fornicator one night in his sleep. Abelard, abruptly neutered but still resourceful, insisted that he and Heloise both take religious vows. Again, Heloise resisted and again she relented. Meanwhile, Abelard had left Paris and lived in a series of monasteries, sowing discord in each one. He even set up his own monastic retreat, the Paraclete, named after the Holy Ghost. It too degenerated into turpitude and chaos.

Eventually, Heloise would restore order there, when she installed her own community of nuns. Abelard went on to greater and greater accomplishment and attendant infamy. His most dangerous writing proved to be a logical analysis of the Holy Trinity, arguing for the separateness of each spiritual entity. Anathema to the Church, this position nearly cost him his life by murder and his soul by excommunication. Ever resilient, he avoided both and at the end of this tumultuous life became reconnected with Heloise, who wrote to him and thus began the legendary exchange. Heloise was prompted to renew contact after reading the very long letter he had written to a fellow monk. In it Abelard related the trials of his life, including his brief but fraught relationship with Heloise. That extended letter, known as his *Historia Calamitatum*, is the background for the first half of this book. Their epistolary exchange, six additional, shorter letters in all, sets the stage for the second half. True to that exchange, Abelard here also gets the last word. Also true to the Moncrieff edition, I insert a brief introduction, which he calls the 'argument', to each letter. Finally, I have taken the entirely personal liberty, because Brittany is Celtic, of setting this poem largely in Ireland, where I spent my early, adult life.

Part One

I

Ezekiel

All we know is a younger monk wrote to the redoubtable Abelard asking for advice. We have no copy of that letter. Nor do we know the monk's identity. What we do have is the woe-is-me tome he received in return. The great man relates in fine, often lurid, detail the story of his life, replete with all its wild vicissitudes, revered one minute, reviled the next, quick as the in and out of breath, over and over again. As a youth, he came up from the country to the city, made his mark, gained instant fame, lost his nerve, went back down, then came back up again. He got his mojo back, his stature, even greater renown. Throughout Europe, he was the man who could enumerate the infinite, then lost it all, won and lost, again and again, his manhood, his way, his wits, the plot, all pleasure, nary a drop, and something else but way back when and memory fails him, ending up on the run, again and again and again, a prisoner of iron terror.

Bruised

I hear you, brother, Hell, but hear me out.
If you are not in Heaven by comparison,
I'll raise a chalice of my blood to you,
A red so dry it makes the deserts weep,
But smoulders purple undertones of damsons,
Stygian and sweet, a delicious black and blue.

Fosterling

I was born on an estuary, part river, part ocean,
A tongue speaking what's been to what will be.
Water sprints over stone, cuts through layers of bog
Like yesterday, meanders through meadow, field and pasture.
The hours as slow as love (or so I'm told),
The decades fast as lust. Then there you are,
Home, the sweet smell of salt air, oblivion.

But first the tidal dither of the present,
The ebb and flow of yes and no and maybe.
Capillaries, veins and arteries, sounds, syllables
And words arrive at the mouth, the very lip
Of silence, then hesitate, wait for the final word.

I was fostered early, sent far away like a letter.
Another child grew in her exhausted womb,
Bright afternoon sunshine evicting morning cloud.

When I returned, I didn't speak to anyone,
Except the angel only I could see.
I listened from my monk's cell high above
The village crossroads, leaning my head like Jesus.

Sounds under a magnifying glass can burn.
Dawn flings off the bed clothes. A bird flaps in the hedge,
Erratic splash of piss, clang of iron on iron,
A poker stirring the dying coals to life,
Clatter of crockery, hiss and spit of a kettle,
Slow bleeding of a pig's serrated squeals,
The creek like a cat creeping tidal in and out,
The tinkling of a cruet and a little bell,
Unbroken voices bending to a baritone,
Clip, clop and clink of carts on the way to the creamery,
A distinctly different pitch coming back empty,
Drone of farmers on the corner smoking,
Replaying Sunday's match, dribbling opinions,
The shutter-banging-eye-opening of shops.
Everything has its price. Our sealed secrets
Steamed whisper by whisper slowly known to all,
Insinuating lilt of gossip, work horse mares,
Their suckling foals, the daily blinkered round,
Breakfast, dinner, tea and supper, the angelus
At noon and six, tolling our hollow hunger,
A swish of soutane, Father pacing the yard,
Caressing the psalms in his well-thumbed breviary.

Dusk. Cacophonous cawing of mocking rooks,
Below the bang of fists, guffaws and curses,
Ring of coins on copper, bottle on bottle,
Low, sullen growl of the feral drink sinking in.
Eleven strikes a squad of clocks, time gentleman
To shunt the bolt and click the till locked.
Uneven whistling thins into the distance.

Deaf footsteps up the stairs, the fewest words,
Their nocturne, usual duet, rat squeak
Of bedsprings, Minerva and Mars at it again.
If only they'd obey a steady rhythm.

Even breathing, in and out of nothing,
Same thing every morning, cock crow, grope
Of sunlight up and up, staining me awake.

Dialectics

Tucked into an inlet on a shallow creek,
A nest in the treetop of the estuary, the abbey.
Monks like brown wrens chirp their lauds and nones,
Their strict discipline chipping away at evil,
Chiselling their bare speech skeletal, the hoot
Of a night hag in the chancel. Their blind dead, hugging
The limestone nave, can feel the touch of morning,
A mother kissing each bowed and tonsured head,
Light streaming through the arched east window, the host
Of the sun mullioned into human portions.

In the opposite direction, brute assertion
Rising from an island in a marsh,
Meek reeds of self-doubt conquered by determined
Rock, the blockish castle. I smuggle myself
Up a clockwise spiral in a winkle shell,
Step by echoing step, me in pursuit of me,
My fear of heights, of drowning in the coffin
Of a shipwreck axed at intervals by light,
Ecstatic at the top, I lean out over
The parapets, let go, soar at the drop, open

My mouth and speak. Or was it he, my angel?
Catapulted like Satan by my zeal up
And over the level midlands, sober lives
Ploughing the same field to the same depth forever,
I landed on another coast and sea entirely,
Black flap of gowns and me holding my ground
On the cobblestones, plunging dialectical
Straight for the sun, Icarus with fireproof wings,
Surviving the flight, the heat, the din, the instant
Fame, the blaze of envy on the master's face,
Wind, a gorse fire, all his acolytes in love.

Test

1. Crux

Abrupt as a thunder clap, the weather turned.
The bones of the air snapped. The cobblestones gave way.
The two, stubby pins on which I'm premised buckled,
And I fell into an even deeper circle of hell.

Mute humiliation. Beached and bloated at low tide.
Fish stench of failure. I'd lost my uphill battle.
Back in the backwater, parochial, alluvial,
Sifting the sediment of what had happened there.

I'd known forever the ruthless ways of water.
Show it some weakness and it's in there. Flooded.
They saw it on my face, drowning in adulation.
They knew the tide would turn and turned on me.

I was a flimsy, wooden jetty in a storm.
He was a granite pier of self-regard.
It's a lucky man who early knows his lust
For love or envy, saves a lot of time.

Saturdays in the dim confession box.
His eminence on one side, me the other,
Right angles looking at him straight in profile,
Always the scrim between sin and absolution.

Night after night submerged in that slimy spiral,
Slipping down flights, counting every step,
One hundred and four, the neatness of ten times ten,
And then that spare digit on each hand and foot.

No rhyme or reason why. I puzzled the wherefore
Of four, cranked the winch of erudition through ones
And twos and threes. Numerology. Theology.
Ratcheting away. The cogs always jammed at the crux.

2. Spiral

North, south, east and west. I'd no direction,
Just the Pagan superstition of peeling an apple
In one, death-defying, Celtic spiral.
Done. No need to choose. It was all possible.

The thought itself propelled me back to front square,
Where damned if I'd not square off, fight my corner,
Not get cornered in an exegetical duel
At dawn. I'd show that fool the real Ezekiel.

The campanile tolled. The crowd congealed.
A conch shell lit from within, opalescent light
On grey facades, the ghosts of gargoyles grinning,
Hounds baying, drooling at the smell of blood.

He won the toss, went first, and wore, the fop,
A bib, a white cravat, to catch every crumb
And drop of his sloppy logic. He made a meal,
A hash, of it. Lot's wife would have been more agile.

His ignominy was my alchemy.
I'd never read the bloody prophet before
That night, when I drank his words in fast, a blur,
Too fast, as the seer received his too clear vision.

Blind to his revelation, before the sun
Dared show its timid face, I struck it rich.
As I had a slash, pure gold, in a piddling river,
It all came to me in an almighty, cleansing cloudburst.

Out of a whirlwind of dung and dust he stepped,
My avatar, that fetishist of four,
And handed me a cheat sheet for the test.
Feign modesty, I thought, kill by degrees.

3. Wheels

I began, thus, quietly, 'Can you see and hear
Ezekiel, his eyes, his ears, there on the Chebar,
Looking north at noon, where a cloud is torched
Untimely to whiskey-honey-rosy sunset?'

Petrified, he peers into that solid proof
Of angels, four, with four heads each, like windless
Weathervanes, ox, lion, eagle, man,
Strength, courage, deadly aim, incarnate love,

Cherubim possessed of the usual four limbs,
Two hands, two hooves, but an unheard of wealth
Of wings, two for flight, two for fig leaf modesty,
As every wing tip kissed a downy other,

Feathered oars built to ply through air like water,
But there was still the stubborn ground to cover.
The scheme of things involved a burning chariot,
Of course, wheels within wheels, divinely inspired,

Each orbit at right angles from its neighbour,
Three hundred and sixty degrees, bedizened, spinning
Rims of sapphire eyes, blue, new-born stars
Looking at us looking through them seeing.

Where the angels went the wheels, where the wheels the angels,
And what is more, they turned not when they went.
Veering off in all directions, they aimed straight,
Undeviating vision at the helm.

Then a throne appeared, a king with loins of molten
Gold but cool as marble. The angels dropped
Their wings in trust. Then a rainbow scythed the sky,
Dazzled beryl, amethyst, prism and arc in one.

Then, lo, the clamour of swans wheeling, unearthly
Love too close to earth, then lightning splitting
The skull, disquiet quiet, then out of that vacuum
Boom, the demiurge, then cloud cover, scar tissue.

Poison

The wind blows fiercest on the mountain top.
Bare rock shivers. Fame is a pumice stone.
It wears you down as it buffs a surface lustre.

More fool me presuming it was over.
I may have won but it had just begun.
Besting the best brings simmer to a boil.

Eyes protruding, head bent, nostrils flaring,
He pawed his patch, hunched his shoulders, snorted.
I could see each hair on his neck stand up and flatten.

Never a man, the cunt, for a bona fide dust up,
He tried to bully his boys into bullying me,
To bust my balls con brio, then to gore me.

But mine was no ordinary wind. The Bora
Broods over snow, seethes over ice, and, when
It can't contain its hate another minute,

Charges with pulverising power, lays waste
To all that dares exist, Medusa's nemesis,
Grinds rock to sand, sand to dust, dust to air,

Erupts in juggernaut gusts as it barrels south,
Rips trees from the earth like so many rotten teeth,
Tiles from roofs, from houses, from foundations,

Dreamy dolphins from the Mediterranean,
Polishes karst, bears down on the coast, Trieste,
Bends every supplicant blade and stem prostrate,

Rolls into the city, snake scours sewers,
Flushes hallways, alleys, nostrils, bowels.
Piss and shit, snot and cum, filth from every orifice.

No place was safe. I battened, hunkered, doubled down,
Bolted my brain, sealed my pores to still the roar.
That slithery beast found out my every crevice.

I shook in my shell, held fast to a pounded rock,
Heard taps, whispers, muffled footsteps leaving
A glass of milk and two macaroons at my door.

Noose

So many pretty mouths mouthing my praise,
Milking words from me like eager seed
Inseminating more words, tomes, my progeny.
I'd have choked if I hadn't been free to run
At the mouth, guttural and bestial, echoes
Of myself, blanks ringing off a cliff face.
Incontinence can pump a great mind impotent.
Nothing is more constraining than chains of gold
To keep their big traps shut, garrotte the pimp,
Pleasure insatiable pups into submission.

I'd started hearing rumours, a leak in the eaves.
Soon roof and walls, the sky, would be down on me.
I needed some modest space between the cheeks
Of polished ladies and corroded trollops,
Some hole, where my bashful fosterling might burrow,
Know a modicum, at least, of total abandon.
Reputation is a double-breasted, brocade
Frock coat buttoned up to the chin and out of there.

Nothing

I don't know. Don't ask me where it came from.
Manna in the desert for God's chosen?
Ezekiel had four limbs just like us,
Four humours, yet he rode the four winds standing
Still. I did nothing to deserve my luck.

She was everything I knew I should desire.
The price was nothing I would ever need.
That edible dew, remember, looked like hoarfrost,
Not intended for the average palate.

For years I've asked was it an accident,
Or did I plan it all myself like Lucifer?

We must be careful prizing truth from pride,
Coagulated cloud, an un-segmented
Mollusc stuck with a pin, flicked from a twisted
Shell, then swallowed with a single slurp,
Tasting of saline otherness, fresh and ancient.

It wasn't me. Her uncle made the overture.
His infamously learned not unattractive
Niece required further teaching, training,
A matter of refinement, rigour, discipline,
Saddle and cinch, bit, bridal and reins for the filly,
A brittle, glittering dome, for his exotic.

Man to man, hand to hand, we struck
A bargain, the terms exact as it was proper,
While nebulous enough to accommodate weather.
She would get tuition, I both bed and board
And the prerogative in fine italics
To chastise the brat whenever I saw fit,
Staking, pruning, coaxing her into flower.

She was deceptive as a lady slipper,
Still green and shy but already endowed with more
Than her fair share of Amazonian pistils.
I'd spotted her before, a mere slip in the shade
Of the cool colonnade, trying to hide behind
Upstart, skinny saplings looking up into
My canopy, hanging on my every word.

I knew it would prove rough and blows were given.
I use the passive here advisedly,
Since all desire for it was clearly on her part,
And I had, after all, avuncular permission
To do needs be for her complete submission,
Cutting remarks, tongue lashings, all to whip her
Into shape, pure strokes of genius, gifts.
Her face burned puce, her skin exhilaration.

She was the quickest study ever, the vixen,
Using fluent Greek and Latin to excite me,
To see her as an eager boy, then bat
Androgynous her lashes, a new declension.
Cut and thrust crossed on coos and sighs beguiled,
Befuddled me until I'd no idea
What I was up to or where the thing was going,
Trajectory, no end in sight, up and down,
Sic and non, fore and aft, until the deed was done.
I didn't see it coming. Nor did she.
Face down, hot tears of gratitude for nothing.

Echo

A slip of the tongue with epic consequences.
My aim off by an inch or less and light years
Of sky, a cosmic sinkhole sucked me down
And back into a black womb quick with stars,
Each one a twinkle in infinity's eye,
While I, a dull speck, circled the same conundrum:
I have to marry but I cannot marry.

Meanwhile, on the forest floor, it grew,
Whisper by whisper, snigger by snigger, huge.
Rumour in a college spreads like the pox.
News of my conquest soon became contagious.
I was the man of the hour hauled to the top
Of the pillar due any second for a comedown,
The explosion of pendulous, pink, voluptuous blooming.

But I'm an eagle, I'd intone, I belong
With other keen, high-minded men, God's raptors
Wed to truth alone, created to soar.
So opined my fanged familiar. My angel knew
How one word puts a stop to all our double talk.
A dead pendulum points true north, six to noon,
No chiming for a virgin's quickened womb,

Until the clock's rewound. I have to marry
But cannot be seen to stoop beneath
My station. It must be quiet as sex for a woman
With a man illiterate of female flesh.
And so, my forked tongue coiled, I asked her straight
To be my wife, to take my hand in non-marriage,
Cold and correct, interring the unbaptised.

And what did I get for my pains but a slap in the face,
So sudden, stinging, sweet I was quite smitten.
The witch could speak the me I couldn't hear
Except when I was he. It was uncanny.
'I will not be your wife, your concubine rather,
On top or under, whatever you prefer,
Just not a statue on an adjacent throne.

And, since you can't consider you, let me.
Would you throw a holy lamb into a pig sty,
A contemplative into caterwauling, nagging hell,
A logician into Bedlam? T'would drive him mad.
I will not snuff out the brightest flame in Christendom.
Besides, I enjoy my notoriety, an aberrant
Woman, choosing risk above security.'

That was just for starters. A banquet followed,
Tasty citations from philosophy and scripture,
Rants against indulgence of the body,
Sober Jerome drunk on quiet, not a drop
Of sound allowed, stoic Seneca alone,
A deer at dawn, when thought creeps up crepuscular.
Didn't she even quote me to me? Scrumptious.

Then on to dessert, no cloying confections, poetry,
But pungent, sharp, the shrew Xanthippe, pouring
From a height (someone had to have perspective)
Abuse on her uxorious spouse, Socrates,
And as a parting shot, letting loose a torrent
On his swollen head. 'Now that will shrink the piss artist.'
His only rejoinder, 'After thunder comes the rain.'

Trinity

1. Three

Only a woman could conceive of such a plan,
Adamantine and then fleece, a perfect lamb,
Her gloating all the sweeter for the bitter
Dose I self-prescribed as divine justice.

I'm built like an ox, low to the ground, but my hide
Is skin and I'd been banging with all my weight
Against that stout oak door, studded with spikes,
Crucified, or so I made it sound to her,

When quick as my temper, click, no turned to yes,
That generous, three-lettered word not we two locked
But open. I cannon balled in, fell splat, flat
On my face, in a very strange place, indeed, married

With a kid on the way. The woman had to go.
She needed family, mine, not her crowing uncle,
Clucking hens, hormonal doting, the estuary,
And wait for the spring tide, when the full moon rises.

The minute the actress mouthed her consent, she ceased
Being she, as we both grew in her belly, one
Two, three, family, no further need for that pair
Of shrivelled crab apples under a stunted tree.

As soft as pollen and quiet as sunset they dropped.
The lightness, the relief. I'd been delivered
Of a weight, straining the fragile web I'd spun.
I could begin now simply to die like other sinners.

2. Two

Then she waddled back, wet and stained with milk,
Her buds bulbous pears bowing a laden tree.
Where had my virgin gone, where I? There,
In that grotto, the newly anointed, swaddled God.

And so, we shoved two beds together, twins,
And got on with our contractual, conjugal truce.
Two stained mattresses, adjacent padded cells,
Two matching coffins, corpses stiff and straight.

One morning I woke, looked toward the far horizon
Of her side. Sunrise soaked the sheet. Ready
Again, I sighed. It did not light a match in me.
I could hear her downstairs boiling and brewing the tea.

I was like Noah righting a Biblical wrong,
But crushed below deck between tits and nuts.
I'd landed on Ararat but didn't speak the language.
The tongue I did would only dig me deeper.

I've the face of a cherub, hence wings as well as hooves.
I'm Michael. I sweep the floor of hell and raise it,
Wipe the smile, my brain, a step behind
My fist. And her going on pummelling dough.

3. One

The blood gushed fast and slow, frozen rose petals.
For years she'd finger that first scar over and over
In a mirror, swear at the ugly reversal of fate.
If you only knew the half, the glass gave back.

I would sit in a corner under a scrupulous lamp,
Inspect the half moons of my nails, and with thumb
And forefinger turn the Manichean pages,
Each one illegible as snow without shadows.

My head is a hammer and chisel. I carve hard truths.
My saint is Denis. I may have lost my manhood
To the sword, but that martyr lost his head,
Then picked it up and walked to preach the word.

Priapic fingers pointed, 'The poor bollox.'
Didn't Leviticus ban rotten figs from the temple,
Lethal as shellfish, but oh their ethereal, total
Loss. There is no man more potent than a eunuch.

I left as the soul leaves the body, there and not there.
We each embraced new vows. She took the veil
And I the cowl. I climbed back up into a shell
The jet of squid ink. I counted every step.

Shamrock

Dank and dark, a dripping cave, but safe
Enough for me to roar, 'I have a body,'
Then hear it ricochet, echo off my ribcage.

Fierce waves, a gale, a cliff reduced to tears,
'There, there,' a heart beats in another room,
Some mother begging her son to stay with her

A little while longer, have a listen to what's out there.
Hush, that swishing in the grass, ages past.
A quail sniffing cress? Maybe Sweeney in a flap?

A mounted voice demands, 'What are you eating?
This is our land.' The stench off a rotting corpse
Uncurls a voice, crooks a knee, tugs a forelock.

'I'm sorry sir. It's only *seamsóg*.' 'Poison,'
Scoffs the agent, 'barbarians,' then trots out
His latest bromide, 'The quicker the better for all,'

And gallops off, the richer for coining that word,
The poorer for not hearing final ones:
'Not *seamair óg, seamsóg*.' (Tongues do get tangled.)

Sorrel, the tart in the bland sauce you slather
On the fish you poach, a soupçon of sour not bitter
Carrion. May you die of your damned shamrock bloat.

That curse rang like the gong they bang for dinner.
It still reverberates, returns like a comet-
Slave-torched-saint, burning up with self-belief

To teach his simple, rooted faith to savages.
He plucked a sprig of three-leaf clover star.
'See these cheeks, this brow. It's love's sweet face.'

If only we'd not put words into his mouth,
To wit those little triplet hearts, each sucking
On the one thin stem, each one the one true God.

If only I'd been self-begetting, the son
And that bugger I called Father axed forever
Down the middle, a suppurating fissure.

At that my supple tongue, a snaky toothpick,
Snuck into the crack between two molars.
Some green stuff had got stuck. With a flick, I freed it.

Amber

You're trapped. You cannot stop once you begin
Smashing plaster statues. She crooks a finger.
(And you feared the virgin dead.) You start again.
Dram after dram, basking in Baltic amber,
Ossified resin. You peer through the heel of a bottle.
A mouth contorts. There must be sound. You're deaf
To all but the insult of that tongue, that spittle.
The concussed room starts checking for its breath.
You're a battering ram hammering sacred mosaics.
Tesserae like tears of bone scatter all over,
The heavens never the same, the picture puzzle
Of the stars, the runic zodiac, apocalyptic.
Your blood is sticky resin. Your piss smoky amber.
You've finally damned yourself to Hell, Ezekiel.

Desert

I had no choice but to repair my body
To some arid place without a drop,
Except my tears and even they were dry.
A blow torch scorched my shadow on the sand.

Or, maybe, since my mind would not stay put,
A hermit's hut in the middle of thick forest,
I'd eat wild herbs, drink icy drafts of water,
Fly from my nest of mud and thatch like Sweeney.

On nothing stronger than the Holy Spirit
I could see white doves fluttering about my bed
Of straw around the clock, an uncut cord,
Sweet nurturance, reattaching me to flesh

I could not feel. No more circuses for me,
No more juggling, mumming in masks, acrobatics,
Barefoot, tiptoe on the sharp point of a pyramid.
I was made rectangular, a plain, wooden coffin.

One morning, a pigeon landed on my sill.
It didn't say my name or bless the day,
When I was born, just looked at me with beady
Eyes and pronounced, 'coo coo roo coo coo,' God's truth.

The sash was raised. I was dozing in a cubicle
Of cotton like a lily, when a bee, eager
To pollinate, brushed against a petal. The curtain
Ruffled, the whole flower aroused. Memory.

The slightest breeze will lift a veil of gauze.
One whorish touch and all our senses humping.
The myth of just one drop, the rush of high tide,
The disgust of low, all that grossness exposed,

The eels, the rats, the writhing and the gnawing,
Sweating, twitching, chiggers drawing blood,
Bloodless maggot phlegm, salutary bloodlettings,
Leeches applied for the balance of my humours.

They multiplied, the parasites. I'd spoken
With my cloven tongue the tongue of everyone.
Flame licked above each over-heated head,
Prophets on fire, each trying to stay sober.

A dozen unweaned lambs in an upper room
At dawn, bearing witness, confessing to their sins,
Sucking on truth, a taste they'd long forgotten,
Each face a sun, blinding and a revelation.

They can see the gleaming temple of the body
Rise from the tomb, the suffocating cassock,
Gagging stench of incense. They can speak at last
The tongues of little children like wind in the leaves

Homeless and cold in winter's shivering branches,
Balls of rag tucked up in tattered anoraks.
Then a wind like a vigorous maid shaking a rug
Scatters that dust up to a heaven no one owns.

Clown

I'd been shorn of all my fleece, all my lies and excuses,
Then left on a mountain somewhere in the Caucasus

In blizzard conditions, the wolves and jackals howling,
Canines like icicles glinting in their mouths,

As they prowled the town below. Exposed and alone,
I was eaten alive by cannibals down to the bone.

Pointed, lupine questions, noses poked in my face,
Sidelong razor glances, poisonous *plámás*

Re-inflating a pig bladder. There was never enough
For them or me of their thin simulacrum of love.

A clown for their carnival, they made it worth it,
Shot from a cannon, a permanent grin. I was hurting

And they could pay, my very own, gilded palfrey,
Celestial transport, conveyance fit for Yahweh.

My sweet, Aeolian voice left widows tickled.
They'd tear off their weeds, fondle my winsome dimples.

Distended with such attention, dying of bloat,
I could not stop grazing on their clover. I'd gloat,

'To be sober and *maith go leor* I've not partaken,
I swear, not a drop of the crayture and still forsaken,

Except by my friends from the upper room, apostles
I've betrayed for a purse of Mammon's sawdust.'

My idol had to die, and I to take the blade
Yet again to my own flesh, gut the sad charade.

West

I'd chased the sunrise so far east, I'd risen
With it, now west of any west I'd known,
Freshly mown hay, a baby's flesh, that scent
On the edge, the wind a scythe, the grass as flat

As a monk at prayer. I look down, towering, sheer,
My bold career soaring like that gull over there,
Where a goat picks his way down to the pounded base,
Shrewd hooves sticking to each chance protrusion.

Fishermen, all comely, one like Jesus, row me
To an island across a boiling, craggy strait.
Our ribbed, leaf-light, empty boat floats high, then sinks
To the gunwales with death in it. Puffins eye me.

Smoke rises from huddled hutches like breath in the cold.
It's dusk at the base of a hill as bald as a crone,
Then golden tresses, molten ocean, the other
Side, the prairie at sunset, and all before me.

Oratory

They like to say it's like an upturned boat,
Right, a boat of stone, sinks the minute you launch it
Out onto water that looks like rock but is
Water. Ah well, let them be, buoyed by their simile.

Above the harbour and below the mountain,
It floats in a lowland swimming with yellow iris,
Nuns in flaring heron wimples, virgins
At the tomb, the vault of my permanent cowl.

The Magdalene once needed me to prick
Her soap bubble syllogisms, always taking off
From therefore. She's a teacher and a healer now.
Not bad, apart from notions and vile touch.

My body came in through that door in the west. I stooped.
My spirit will slip through that window in the east,
Ocular and inward splaying light
Presenting, a soft fontanel from a fossilised womb.

Fishermen all day row in an element with too much
Give, by night trudge foreign, too firm land.
Litters of pilgrims have sheltered here between
Day and night, the ocean and that haloed peak.

As we pass the petrified hours below just waiting,
We may as well observe, since there's little else
To do, the miracle of how it all balances, fits,
A skull without one fleck of sophistic mortar,

So tight to the wind and rain it might be fish scales,
An imbricated glittering, but it's not.
To name it is to cut dull, corbelled stone,
Ever leaning, edging up, their faith in increments.

Blood

What with the fighting without and fear within,
And fear without and fighting within, I'm dead
From the war I live to fight day and night, night and day.

The convex mirror of nightmare, rotund grotesques
In a blink deflate. The sun is a staved-in navel,
The lids of my eyes pried open by a crowbar.

Ogres *stravaiging* through some city in hell
In a flash turn lean, the rabbit warren linear.
Panthers prowl round and round a rectangular cloister.

The stone of the starless tomb rolls back to morning
Rain, each drop at a defiant tangent
To the earth each one must hit, submit

To the curve of the foul river I crossed last night
Evaporating as I wake to daylight
Already in spate, eddies of opaque, poisonous plots.

I am their abbot. The loaves and fishes multiply
For me in the refectory. When I bend my neck
To suck a bone, I'm Dionysus. A blade hovers

Like their curses. A hare sucked the udder of a cow.
That very night a hag was splattered with blood.
Now, our churn is impotent. There's no more butter.

I starve myself on empty speculation:
Meat larded with deadly ceps, mead spiked with cyanide,
My face in the chalice flushed from belladonna,

And everywhere the ineradicable chancre of simony.
Boys pay for their sins, on their knees for a *te absolvo*.
Whores skitter and gnaw for a bleeding dose of juniper.

Locked to keyholes, translating whispers, their tongue
Bedding our Latin, poxing our civilisation,
Erupting all over, my skin awash in vowel pustules.

It's got so bad to take a breath is suicide.
Yet I'll be damned if I'll commit the sin,
Give them the satisfaction. Never. Damn them.

The time isn't ours to decide, nor the place, places,
Cells, huts and caves, the few faces in which I lodge
My trust the worst, convex, concave, the deformity

Is me, Cain on the run, in the valley of the dry bones
All alone, wetting parched lips with unharkened prayer,
My very persecution proof I'll rise again.

The son is the father. The father is the son.
Nailed to that chiasmus, I trust only the ghost,
Who has nothing to lose or gain. Thy will be done.

Part Two

I

Gentian

So much time and so much space, centuries traversed from
Medieval France to here and now. At last, she can breathe
again, be quietly herself, hear ordinary sounds, see ordinary
sights, take innocent, daily pleasure in a flower, a bird,
emerge from the total eclipse of anhedonia, his religion. At
last she can feel the sun on her skin, as at her birth. Once
more, she begins.

He, who goes by Abelard, may well have etched into
metallic immortality his image of the woman he called
Heloise. She is not that person; but she will never have
the acid tongue or bite to incise the mordant truth they
shared. No matter. If she can help to hatch another's life by
speaking one word as warm and fragile but curiously tough
as a bird's egg, she'll live with that.

Glacier

Dear Peter, I don't know why I'm writing to you,
Except to say I spotted a gentian today,
My first of the season. Where I live now, that's news.
Winter would not give up. Spring was so delayed
We feared another ice age, and now blue sky
Has pushed through a gryke in the cloud underfoot, a shy
Azure, still stunned by the trauma. I had to write,
Speak for the soul behind the face. Eurydice
Did it herself, without the aid of Orpheus
And his lyre, finally arrived at this austere
Place, this cool, reflective, lunar surface.
No more fevers, shivering, rigours, viscous rivers
To cross. No need to look back, reply. After Hades,
The warmth of the sun is quite enough. Love, Louise.

Cincture

The forceps pressure in that birth canal.
Think of a leaf exploding in petrified air,
Hard long before land rose from the primal hush
Of water. Embedded skeletons, coral and sea urchins
Wink as I rotate my sharp tectonic
Plates, finesse a buttress, shoot through an arch
On a rush, fold my cranial bones, still flexible
As the future, into a flower, a lotus position,
Then crown, rocket into now, begin to breathe.

The labour it takes to birth yourself from Hell,
Sister, daughter, handmaiden, wife. You wear
A chemise bound by a cincture to keep it together
And bleat, 'When you left me, you took me with you.
For not with me but with thee alone was I me,
At thy sole behest, I'd be blessed with non-existence.'
Passive aggressive confessions. Abbess to Abbot,
Father, brother, master, spouse, such fissures.
Every day I slip through a crack, go back to Heloise.

Virago

Who in God's name do you think you are? Abelard?
With your head so far up the arse of the Middle Ages,
You'll not have heard the letter you sent that wretch,
Who came to you for succour (the better to seek
Refreshment from a cesspool), has gone viral.

Even I, every inch the Victorian headmistress now,
And who well might be the abbess-scribe at the ruin
I pass each day on the boreen down to the shore,
Where I walk, weep, pick winkles for supper, have read it.
My novices too. I can tell by how they look at me.

Don't get me wrong. I'm charmed by your allusion
To Xanthippe. What pissed me off was a sin
Of omission, no mention of Medea, epitome
Of downy femininity gone hard.
Under you I achieved the peak of notoriety.

I saw you on the telly once. You were walking
A cliff walk, talking the talk. You were asked had you any
Remorse, amends to make. You named your names
With the blurry deliberation you'd put into putting
Your jiggling key in the lock locked. I listened hard

For sorry. Now I've choked on that anachronism
You put into my mouth in print. I never said
You'd end up in Bedlam, that medieval asylum.
If your aim was making me look bad, I'm flattered.
If you screwed up, we can't have that now, Abelard.

Heaven

I saw this particular birdwatcher on Abbey Hill.
We often chat in passing. We're both from away.
Today, she looked like she could fly to Africa.
After too long a silence (she'd feared the worst), just now
She'd heard a song thrush and before my eyes
Thrust out her chest and returned to the bliss of listening

To that flute, each note the chaste hand of dawn,
The caress of dusk, taut fiddle strings under a supple
Bow, percussive beak stabs, rivulets of trill,
Mesmeric repetitions, a thrumming mantra,
Vibrations on the tympanum of then,
Whenever such flesh music happens to happen for you.

'Did you see it?' 'No.' 'Are you sad?' 'Not really.' Just once,
That's all it takes, the sight and sound in unison,
The creature and its voice, bound for life. And it works
Two ways. Looking down on a river in flood, you can hear
A Bach concerto, the flying apart, the drifting back,
The fit, the flow. 'I saw him.' 'I know. I'm waiting.'

Barter

The short cut proved the long way round. Mid-summer,
Insomniac sun. She ambled through the market.
Throngs pressed the flesh. Is this salmon firm and fresh?
These strawberries plump and sweet, as ripe as June?
Crubeens and chickens, carrageen moss and peas.
The price went up according to the depth
Of hunger in a voice. 'Cheap flowers,' 'cheap flowers,'
Hypnosis, the sellers' siren sing-song roses.

He undressed her with a glance, the burly butcher,
And, as he dressed a rabbit, they danced a minuet.
One hand grabbed the neck, the other the hindquarter,
Then wrung it like a wet, gutted rag. A snap,
Two knuckle cracks, a quick slit in each hock,
And like a gentleman removing a fine, leather glove
In one clean stroke all that soft, protective fur
Slipped off the long, lean, torso, a kit on a hook

Drying off from a swim. She reached her destination
Around midnight, watery light, cobblestone cloud.
Threshold and lintel the jaws of a skull, and inside
Those rooms, the catacombs in winter, a one bar
Electric fire. Hot whiskey. Narcolepsy.
She woke all alone on an autopsy table, the sheet
A slab of marble, a wild animal in her pelt.
3 AM. Ice cut through ill-fitting shutters. Morning.

Midges

In the beginning, he sang for me alone.
Preposterous, of course. Against all logic.
Standing room only. Legions of lip-synching fans,
And only I could hear him, his little Gnostic.

Caught in a downpour of sound, I was the rain.
One note and I was dew assumed by the sun.
But only if my eyes stayed unconstrained.
I'd be pinned to the ground by his, if mine were open.

We study the body. We listen to the soul.
Disciples radiate a certain faith, each ray
Of his gaze their star entire, mainlining the gospel
According to him, gored on the horns of cerulean eyes.

Astigmatic, I could see how he saw them,
Saw us, as a flash crowd of dithyrambic gnats
Obscuring his view of the luminous cloud where some
Reside, intoning, atoning for all that is not

Ultraviolet light. At that my scorched retina
Detached. I saw black, swam in a swarm of sperm,
Roman centurions sent to inflict the stigmata.
It took just one to nail him to the podium.

Yet again, crucifixion, resurrection. Tedious,
Rising and shining for yet another bash at it,
A twisted genius bearing the sign of the cross
On his blazing brow. Their kisses turned to ash.

What rose from that unholy mess was Judas.
I lost my soul to save it, tossed the last straw
On the pyre and lit it. No Phoenix, Jesus
Wept. *Mea culpa*, etcetera, *mea maxima culpa*.

Theology

You had to be extremely careful then
lowering the needle onto vinyl
not to scar the new moon face.

Prosaic tapes were slow,
took time to think before they spoke,
got all tied up in knots.

Already obsolete,
full moon CDs are 33s
compressed to a faux clarity
designed for OCD,
at the tip of a finger replay, replay, replay.

'Blue-oo-oo-oo,'
or is it, 'Blue-oo-oo-oo-oo,'
or better still, 'Blue-oo-oo-oo-oo-oo,'
3 or 4 or, heaven, 5?

As if Pythagoras were Jesus,
number your saviour,
order imposed on a voice like wind chimes.

Rock hopping through a forest,
shaft of light to light,
drowning in the shadows.

Lapis beads fall through your hands like water.
How to carve a river?

And doesn't one 'oo' morph into a 'you,'
a go-with-the-flow, hippy embryo

now skipping and repeating herself,
Joni,
my old, grey Camry with a slipping clutch?

Oh to be back in the then new, smooth, blue Volvo,
a mother and son on mute,
the audible clatter of tapes
going round and round a truth.

Wistful melisma.
Manic syncopation.
A languid hand on a thigh in a dream.
Paroxysms contracting at the point of impact.
A gin and tonic, two.

Indigo tattoos staining the skin of generations to come.
The whole story. I still haven't got a clue.

Sky stencilled onto cloud.
A Wedgewood platter struck by lighting, shattered,
stitched up with glue,
another oval dawn.

One nail strikes another nail
directly on the head, sinks the sin
so far in steel can't but feel
a proto finger or a toe.

Gagged and trussed of her own volition,
the magician's assistant
(without whom there would be no show)
steps into the coffin.
The lid comes down, the blade,
1 and 1 are 2, then Hallelujah
the one, lithe woman rises from the grave unscathed.

Packed into the pit, a groundling,
swallowed by touch, you're free to feel
that brush on the inside of your skin,
a far cry from a full-term wind,
enough to make you two again,

A childish prelude to a very adult song.
Tentative fingers press expectant keys.

Then one day, there is nothing
for it, inside out, a holy show,
but to pray the not you in you, living
ambiguity, will just continue to breathe
your blood and grow.

The weather turns. You're a cirrus cloud,
a mare's tail, swatting flies and gnats,
the slightest threat to it,

your posture too. You tiptoe
over burning coals, a kiln
firing the final glaze on porcelain,
Limoges.

Soon signals from a semaphore, a distant shore,
grow closer, clearer, almost regular.

Communication from a star,
Morse code for there is life out there,
deep in the cosmos of the flesh,

exploding as the rocket takes off,
blasts through all your strata,
every melt-down and re-glaciation,
touches down on the touchscreen

of now, opens its one, white, minute eye,
unfolds its five (you count them) sapphire digits, yes,
a genuine, alpine gentian jewel
on this denuded surface.

Oh Blue, the only god I know.

II

Jeremiah

Despite his better judgment, Abelard writes back. He must.
The woman's soul is in peril. And, although she refuses to
acknowledge it as true, they are still married in the eyes
of God. As he, Abelard, sees it, the woman is damned by
subjectivity, a prisoner of intellectual vanity and carnal
proclivities. Why now, on the cusp of eternity either way,
recite an interminable litany of post-lapsarian nature,
stunted flowers, inarticulate birds, she who once consorted
with the sky.

And she won't let up, never could. She never learned,
as he did (oh so young), we are nothing but the servant
of The Word, not cowering words, the one, imperial sun
bearing down on us. If only she could accept the gift of
being modest, selfless, virtuous, pure, woman, the Virgin
Mary. If only she'd accept how he, in the name of Him, had
no choice but to punish and diminish her, save her from
grandiosity.

Jeremiad

If only I had spoken my own words
not the Word, I'd be accountable for them.
But who goes to Hell for the sins they commit in dreams?

It's well for some flouncing around in the latest
heretical fashion, flaunting their freedom of speech,
while I, draped and veiled, suffocate like a wife.

Every time the first time you are hit, the voltage
of his touch, as He parts your hymen lips,
the shock of having words put in your mouth,
fish vomit, metallic, the slit soldered white-hot shut.

Don't the sun and moon, the king and queen of the sky,
come and go like slaves at his capricious will,
serene and beaming one minute, glowering the next?

Each time the first time you give birth, an armoured
voice, words issuing from the abyss,
gutting you articulate, the deity no less
decreeing you were his before you were

your mother's. Teleology. The seed complete
in her contingent womb, and she no virgin.
From the beginning, some woman's gross abuse
of choice left me with no choice but to warn
idolatrous harlots of their master's wrath.

We plant ambition to reap the thorns of bitterness.
The wheat of solid nourishment grows elsewhere.
Our stomachs rumble, echo like abandoned silos.

We spurn the extended, almond wand of grace
to run our Jezebel hands up and down the snaky
stems of grapevines, greedy for every last drop,
then wake in a vineyard of skeletons alone and parched.

Stubble

Paradoxical, I know, addressing an individual
to declare the personal irrelevant as weather
compared to Hell's eternal conflagration.

And furthermore, you are not you. You are
the mother of his only child, his son, scion
of the long and chosen line you choose to imperil,
the only sound tree in an orchard torched by blight.

Air is treacherous and root systems incestuous.
Your impious words spread like locusts, fungus, mould.
I leave to climb the mountain, to receive the word,
and you far below forge a golden calf from your belly,
deify a flower, its petals the Pentateuch.

You are no more than a hacked and stunted stalk
of corn stubble, rows of tombstones hoary with frost,
so numb you no longer feel your obsolete roots,
and with the stiff limbs of your failing memory
will never again feel your tassels nuzzled by wind.

Do not casuistically twist my words like the wool
you spin by a dampened fire to ward off the
inevitable. You have every right to wake (well, no)
mornings and cling to adulterous clouds of dreams,
as they slip from your arms, go back to the little wife.

Like mistaking a lightweight for a man of substance,
you elevate, inebriated with ephemera,
an albeit alpine gentian, *gentiana verna*,
(its entire species under threat of extinction)
into the blue washed, bloodshot eye of some Lord
God Almighty, looking down the morning after on
some moth, some woolly moth, freezing on naked tundra.

Dust

It was He who administered that stock slap on the wrist.
I would never be caught spoiling the rod by sparing it.
He catapulted a pebble at your thick skull
and you fingered the pock mark forever like a crater.
I'd have hurled your corpus at a dry stone wall,
toppled your wobbly pretensions, your draughty theories.

It was not me. It was you with your guilty fasheen
begging the heavens to open up and rain down
hail like clenched fists, dent your vanity like tin,
release a torrent, hose down your polluted skin,
your slut eyes painted big and bold with kohl
like Cleopatra, now smeared with tears of soot.

You took one bite of a not-yet-ripe green apple,
doubled over with cramp, then farted your opinions
in my face and you expect me not to raise a hand
against such flatulence, banish the stench of ignorance.

There sits the judge, thumb up or down, his quaint
binary, there the victim, a glittering diadem
of certainty. Only the accused bears the fruit of confusion.
Our ever ramifying, rarefying deliberations
on good and evil are so many leaves that twist
in the wind, glint in the sun. Only He sees the whole,

specious tree uprooted without warning. It hit,
fast as the wind, slow as a glacier, an avalanche
of long-dammed, pent up water. Who, I wonder,
opened the floodgates and released such anger?

Tossing boulders in the air like marbles, letting them
drop, where they will, bomb a new configuration,
castle and hovel, king and commoner one roaring,
raging, dull quartz mirror bearing no reflection
of a man I thought I knew, though out of a corner
I saw you cowering before some monster, who was not
me. I too am dust in his whirling tempest.

Milk

'Hail, Mary, full of grace the Lord is with thee.'
I should try, when addressing a virgin-nun, to be Gabriel,
not glum Jeremiah, but find, when I'm beside
myself, I'm graceless. Plus, you still haven't got a clue
just how blessed you are, the mother of an only
child, a son, who comes begging for your intercession.

He who sows opens the hand of trust and throws
his seed so high up it nearly flies into the sun
and burns. Most of us, born wingless, have the luck
to fall onto forked-over ground, the shallow grave
of every birth, sink greedy roots, and grow
to accept the sun and moon as penitent spouses,
the abbot of light, the abbess of night and morning.

I, for my sins, am a starling, went straight for my star,
was snatched in mid air by an eagle. Now I need
some woman, a midwife, to free me from his clutches,

for he's just a man, and you know how men can be.
Didn't Martha and Mary together make Jesus remember
himself and shower down tears on the sand of Lazarus,
the cadaverous lad brought back to blooming life.

Such is the feminine power of appearing powerless,
the persuasion of cool mist on a fevered brow.
Sure, you might have kept rash Jephthah, blind to all
but ambition from making the vow that would see him see
his daughter, his only, and do what he had to do.

We have to play the part we're given. You're Abigail.
Didn't you coax two eejits at each other's throats
to put their blades back in their pockets and suckle,
one at each dug, like good little cubs on mercy?
Pray for me sister, as if you were my mother.
'Now and at the hour of my death. Amen.'

III

Crab apples

It was real as breeze block, the house they occupied on the
Irish Sea not far from Dublin's underwater luminescence.
Their bodies intersected briefly there. The point the
compass needle pierced soon rounded into flesh, a third
dimension, Astrolabe, their son. He is all she thinks of now,
as he navigates his future by the sky he studied as a child
for any hint of order, the constellations other children go to
in their dreams to play with bears and lions. But there were
too many stars for him to count, too many points of view,
and each one absolute, from the coolest blue, faraway father
eyes, to his mother's saccharine, vermillion jelly boiling
over in the kitchen on the hob.

Why couldn't his sun and moon like other parents share
in silence the one, small circle of existence, not talk, talk,
high flown comet talk, then low down lightening, brooding
silence…he'd count the miles until it boomed, thunder
shattering the dome, new blood on old, relief, meteor
dust coming to rest on his skin, as he stares at the ceiling
stitching up the latest breach, slow motion looping of the
gleaming needle, in and out, cat gut or silk, who cares? Just

another badly sutured promise to break like the neck of a bird. Soon he'd be left with the moon alone. His sun would vanish. How he'd miss that dangerous radiance, days when his mother would fold into her flesh, go totally dark and cold. She too might never come back.

Tongues

It wasn't as you'd have me in the story,
pregnant and recumbent on a palanquin,
above it all from Paris to the Loire,
then buoyed on the shoulders of that river, all the way
west to Brittany, a tongue of land, a duchy
with its very own, as the French would have it, *langue*.

It was Dublin, a taxi to Kingsbridge, the Limerick
train, his Austin mini, cloying pipe smoke
and an airtight monologue, all along the estuary's
lapping lip in the kingdom of garrulity,
on and on to the crossroads he kept calling 'home,'
halfway between the mouth and the faceless deep,

which God in another yarn breathed upon, dividing
water from waters. Mine broke on the Irish Sea.
Delivered of the myth my body was my own,
I went back down, our baby boy in my arms,
wrapped in a blanket of woolly sunshine, down
where the light off the water wavers salt and fresh.

Holding tight to the future, I kept slipping back to the past.
Barely in bud, barely out of the car and the postmaster,
God's truth, was on me, digging in my envelope

for news. Will the heifer deliver? But it wasn't those shovel
hands. It was that tongue raking spit in my face.
Drowning in rapids, I got not a word, being pawed

in mime and no one to hear the foreigner scream.
I forget if you were with me. You were passive as dust
the minute the *sidhe* would gust from the house, sweep you up
in their apron, down to the kitchen, the land under wave.
This time, when they heard the car, they swooped down and snatched
(I can still feel the tear) the hatchling from his nest,

took him under their wing, up to their eyrie, then started
to pass him around, a trophy for the team,
each seeing their face in still molten gold, unfocussed
eyes, 'There, there *mavoorneen*,' licking the calf
with diminutives, the mother tongue, family
to steady his shaky start. 'Hush, hush, you're home.'

Then a feather brushed my arm. 'You're tired. Get some rest.
You'll be on tap soon enough.' The hands of experience
were on my breast adjusting the angle of nipple
to mouth, then the thrill as that tongue suctioned survival.
His trusting face looking up at mine also blind
to how mothers must see a motherless, new mother,

otherwise free. But privacy was porous there
as sand on a floodplain. At the crack, he'd be in the room,
teacup in hand, then we'd tour the townland together,
the abbey on the Shannon, ruinous with pregnant
mounds we'd tiptoe around to get to the family
plot. 'Here's my father, my sons, their sons and me,'

on and on. 'And where will I be?' I asked. 'With your people,'
banished to the back of my mind but never more with me
than on that train going back the way I'd come down,
only faster. The rain-streaked windows offered no
reflection of what I'd become, just water, more water.
The tongue that swaddles us swallows us home to silence.

Husbandry

Medallions of cat shit,
dandelion floors,
the Irish Sea a meat cleaver
hacking under the scullery door,
cracked quarry tiles the colour of dried blood.

All summer long, the earth was on a binge.
Tut-tutting noses pressed against our glass.
The rain poured down.
The grass shot up as hay.
Inebriated weeds staggered.
The flood began to rage.
Waves crashed against our big bay window
on a rampage.

And then it was September.
The guy up from the country with the scythe,
A few quick bob to hone and mow
the Dubs back to the garden wasted.
The heavens took a pledge.
The boy got shorn for school.

Throughout, the man of the house was at the helm
braving a livid ocean of ink.
Now high and dry, a week at best,
Noah strode down the gangplank
and off into town, a mighty thirst upon him.

The wrath of God receding,
left sorting through the flotsam,
a tortoise shell barrette,
the rare fine day I let my hair down,
seaweed swayed, recovering a dream,
old toys the boy thought lost forever fallen
from the sky, the archer's bow and arrow
stars, to see you through the darkest days
no fickle, loner rainbow
scads of huge fire-fly ruby
marbles strewn by some giant
under our unpruned tree
like Christmas.

Who can resist a windfall?
Who doesn't purse insulted lips
at every loss of innocence?

So it begins again,
the lessons, labour, learning, trying
to redeem some sweetness from a tart,
too often bitter, harvest,
threshing the present, winnowing
the rotting and the rotten from
the ripening and ripe,
the ground picked clean, the kitchen coming down
with crab apples.

Full on, the tap, splatter and splash,
washing each bruised and blemished gem,
topping, tailing stem and blossom ends,
then plop into the stockpot
brimming, boiling, calming to a deadly
simmer, however long it takes to reduce
fibrous fruit to pulp.

You fetch a witch's broom,
set back-to-back, a bit apart,
two rough hewn chairs, then rest
the handle on the matching rails akimbo,
suspend the jelly bag,
place a crock below to catch what's vital,

now pour everything you've got,
that cauldron's guts,
into a sieve of muslin scrupulosity,
so close a weave it fine tooth catches
every lie like lice. A slog.
You have to work
at doing nothing only let
the painfully distended udder drip
its blood-laced pus.

Do not press or squeeze or stir
the verbiage. Like willing grief to end
the end will be forever murky.
It has to be let drip, wan sun
through cloud, and, when you've not a drop
of patience left, suddenly it stops
breathing. Ready.

Light glints off the copper pan,
snoozes in the scalded metal spoon,
Stay cool. Measurement, precision, the ratio of sour
to sweet, sustained attention
make the difference in the end between
it all coming together
somewhere, somehow in the muddled middle,
and caramalised hate or flat existence.

Just keep on stirring
to prevent the syrup sticking, scorching.
It's tai chi. Skim off the foam, every speck of spume.
You'll be fit to die before you think you see
a silky clarity, but test it, test it,
dip and lift the spoon. If time keeps dripping like a clock,
you're not there yet, until you see
it sheet like Creation in the wind,
beg for form, the twinkling firmament
of readied jars, sterilised and hot as comets.

In the beginning, so the end,
you seal the tomb with paraffin,
toy soldiers on the pantry shelf,
a long dead garnet star reborn
the happy pink-red of cracked nipples,
after all that nursing,
sweet, celestial jelly, finally.

Scattery

Putt, putt of the outboard motor,
lap, lap, the odd slap, on the hull,
fiddle strings plucked,
the ribs dilate,
waves stronger than they look.

A shower of light or shafts of rain?
It depends on the clouds
in his sky, mine.

His fine, soft day is my snow melting.
His home is the eye-level, dwindling dot
of just a day trip. Full stop.

Mine is the star I swim to nights,
when his son nods off
and the sky is jet and I can't resist
the twinkling of that tune,
'Oh, I wish I had a river I could skate away on,'
back to where the ice is still unscarred.

This estuary is a vice.
The more it expands the tighter it gets
like a clan.

Oh, I wish I were a river
and there weren't two sides,
just the one body
of water keeping it together,
as the air keeps the gleaming stars
in touch with dusty asters.

Islands need islands.
Skirting Scattery in a downpour,
medieval piety through isinglass,
the sun begins to break out
on his face and I know
we're in for a rainbow.

There was this saint, he begins,
who vanquished an invading nun
with the off-putting habit of sucking
on coagulated blackberries,
staining her tongue,
tainting the holy ground,
tempting his monks with a tiny taste of sin,

when all your woman wanted was to lie with him
cold as a corpse on the choir floor forever, I snort.

When he went to Heaven, his brothers dug
a grave for his bones in the nave,
now in ruin. When she went to Hell,
he dug a shallow hole at the low-tide line,
let the ocean do the dirty work.

Oh, I wish I were a river,
this very one, the Shannon,
Sionnan, she with the power
to let the silly man drive
his cattle over her dry bed and yet resist
(more power to her)
the urge to swallow his herd holus bolus
into her high tide maw,

At which my boatman breaks into a ditty,
'Oh haste and leave the sacred isle
Unholy bark ere morning smile,
For on thy deck, though dark it be,
A female form I see.'*

'Oh, I wish I were a river so long
I would teach my feet to fly'
glide all the way home
in parallel lines, an abbess and an abbot
feasting beatific on each other
deep in Clare,

limpid Clare, my window
onto solid ground
no sooner there then gone,
the blinds drawn down.
'We mustn't be late for our tea,'
he chirps, pointing his beak
south for home.

Once I'd been away for far too long.
Just off the boat, only back,
I popped into a bakery and asked for bread.
Not a crumb in my mouth
and I tasted that loaf.
My tongue was home.

And I was starving
like that Arctic tern
flapping above our heads,
keeping her tryst
in the breeding grounds
of summer.

*from *Moore's Melodies*, 'Saint Senanus and the Lady' by Thomas Moore

Whiskey

Twinkling, ice blue, cut glass eyes designed
To hide the blast of the furnace, red-hot, molten.
Cold as Lucifer, he drew those bevelled diamonds,
Lowered the wheel and carved that play of reflection,
Each glittering occasion, anthracite in the grate,
A brass hod, candelabras, Waterford chandelier,
Kaleidoscopic men in suits. Black agate
Eyes spinning alive in disco balls of terror.
Pilgrims flock to the holy well, kneel and sip the water
Of life, drink a dry drunk dead of being the angel,
Flogging his demons sober, until tongues of fire
Appear on a silver salver and speak through crystal

Shards they'd extract with tweezers. He took it neat,
The blood moon refracted through each once, brilliant facet.

Wimbledon

The kitchen table was our grass tennis court,
him one side, me the other, fierce back and forth.

So essential each to each, we could seem like the same
whizzing ball, not two competitors, the game.

Of course, he was McEnroe and I was Borg,
intoxicated play versus the sober slog.

Or was it the opposite? Now and again, too often,
predictable antics, some random deviation

from the norm. His serve, 'Alas, it's verse, jejune.'
'But it's satire, that's deliberate,' my return,

then his lofty lob, 'We must beware what we mock.
Words can make the thinnest of fare even thinner, or
muck.'

His thick-and-thin contradiction then was beside
the point. He'd won the point and we were tied,

when the child in his highchair let out a roar on the sidelines.
No flip of the coin. Naturally, the duty was mine,

and just when I was about to broach that breach
in reason, for reasons beyond my ken I reached

down deep and took my game to another level.
Back in the days of tea and scones, when Wimble-

don was in black and tennis whites on television,
and men were men and women proper women,

this was a long shot but I couldn't resist,
'Is it because you have a penis and I have breasts?'

I knew he relied on my groundstrokes, my boring logic;
but I was addicted to his high-flying scholastics.

I hit him with a shot ripped from his book, 'We're family,
right, like the holy family, the holy trinity?'

The saint patiently explained each was one in three,
a whole composed of discrete, quite separate entities.

Aced it, brought my very flesh back to feeling queasy
some wind might uproot the lily pad in and of me.

My life depended then on our flattery rallies,
'What a lovely volley.' Live with the lies or die

from your echo's lack. I'd met my match, thwack, thwack,
match tough, tougher with each murderous over and back.

The tension mounted. I chanced a backhand, 'I've tied you
up in your own knots' to 'Have you now, Delilah?'

Deadly drop shot quiet, the heart of the forest, repartee
over. Then wind sheer, a micro-burst, toothpicks for trees.

Skin and bone metal chairs either side of the slumped umpire.
As each sat there plotting the fifth set in the war,

he scored the winner with topspin, 'Sin is all intention.
Did you mean evil or succumb to whim?' Whose tantrum

was it, his or mine? All the smashed, wooden rackets,
scattered bone and gut, each tightly strung nerve end snapped.

Who did it? Who will finally go to Hell? The scoundrel
with his head in his hands or she with the icy smile?

Empty

Bang goes the solid brass, spring-loaded slot. Thud
goes the post, daily after shocks. The walls shudder.

The plaster's gashed, the floorboards gouged, Braille
You'd read with your hands, if only you could feel.

Rip up the scutch grass, chuck the spent dirt, start over.
Lay down for drainage a bed of jagged cinders.

The glare of night, stray animals, strobe lights, corpses,
Day dark, a crack in tarmac. Noon, and the sun drops.

A stone sarcophagus, a metal cash box frozen.
No luck, licking the rim, stroking the lock open.

Mirrors, contortions, legs and arms in knots, all to see
up close the lesion, the rash, the pus, depravity.

Flahoolagh with seed, the wind made a girl a mother.
Wheat shot from her breasts to feed another's hunger.

Whiplashing from wall to wall, the cat, epileptic,
saved from herself, wrapped static in a blanket,

a straightjacket, four walls, for your own good,
happy pills that make you manic, cattle prods,

soporific sessions with the shrink. The great man
listens, thinks, picks little bones out of his salmon.

You have to move, stuck in a queue, you almost break
its neck, stride out Dun Laoghaire pier and shriek.

No gaps, once words continuous and green as grass.
Now arid, mute, the underside of Genesis.

'Being with child,' that frail preposition a stem,
lifts a face up to the sun, done with the womb.

The gradual, merciful melt of today's stiches.
Back then they were, then not, concave, a pit.

The child's dewy lips rubbed by an unguent thumb,
like father, like son, the steep cost of exorcism.

The aspergillum sprinkles its dust on coffins,
as though the dead came back to life through Latin.

The blow master inflates his malleable bubble,
inspects its shape, rotates his rod, doing his job.

Sleepy but no sleep or appetite, edgy lethargy
the ghost of a cat prowling a house long empty.

Wide awake, you pray to the waves up the road, return
me home, let me feel the elation of numbing ocean.

Uisce beatha, the water of life, whiskey.
His sober, parting shot, 'You'll be nothing without me.'

IV

Lazarus

He, Peter, has to hand it to her. She's done it, stripped him
of every sleight and feint, ripped off his mask and held up
a mirror. Finally, he sees not a cherub or a demon, sweet
extremes, but a pure bollox. At least he now has naked
truth on his side. She will never know what such a flaying
feels like, ever protected by perfidious, perfumed flesh.
Putrid and creased as a rotting corpse, he is ambrosial
within, poised for rebirth. She may have reduced him to
a dry drunk, windbag, pervert, on his worst day, when his
heart was breaking truly, vampire nun, but no, he's merely
incontinent now, Ezekiel's golden chariot is on its way.

Interrogation

I'm sorry, but I did not hare off to a monastery.
I limped like a pup smartly kicked into submission.
Crossed the godless bog to sup at trough of pig-swill.

From my earliest, unweaned days, I've had this genius
for battering attachment into flat abandonment,
shot by shot, whatever it takes to kill, fill the void

I slip into, fire down the gullet, a sleek otter whelp,
down the steep, muddy bank, then deep into my element,
swimming slick as a fish into Leviathan's maw,

Pandemonium boiling up from that gut below,
and every hell since, cold gusts through the swinging doors,
ghosts up from the country in Sodom and Gomorrah.

Guppies tucked into a snug, a dim aquarium,
musk of wet wool, acrid, too sweet blanket of Woodbines,
swaddling. The toughest cord to cut is smell.

That litter of scrofulous, scabrous, rank hangers on
just about hanging on to my every slurred, surgical word,
cirrhosis faces flushed, ignited with spiders,

out of hand, to the onlooker, no doubt, in my control,
the fallout of nuclear loss, each halting tick-tock
of the juggernaut clock until it stopped. Time to quit

living off dying embers, some amber autumn
elsewhere, not osmotic dusk through frosted glass,
'The same again, curate,' my one bit of sun, Jameson,

eclipsed. Black out. The interrogation room,
scalpel questions in the kitchen, impregnable
pyjamas, that pietistic wrap, the smug gob on her.

I spared, apparently, nothing, from furniture to dust,
wasted not one empty word. They could not matter less
on the ocean floor, where the waters take a vow of silence.

Trying

Sobriety's like light for the blind, who see
for the first time, say, those salt and pepper shakers,
the perfect couple, the too white cloth, the grey
off the sea and me down to take the air, recover,

adjust to the glare, how objects wear a halo,
those containers little lighthouses, the sea with its surface
tension. Our best behaviour hides a reef below,
scorch marks on linen, your wine with its meniscus.

Convex? Concave? (I'd begged you to drink.) No or yes?
The roller coaster made me dizzy, all a blur.
I was trying to find my balance, a single focus
for two divergent eyes. One saw only inner

fact, a drought so severe my soul was cracked mud,
the other outer rapture. I'd get drunk on colour
or its purer lack. Your merlot was menstrual blood,
and me with my glass of intoxicating tap water.

I'd sworn not a word, a drop, would pass, let alone
a brotherly kiss, my lips. I was trying to heal
a festering wound, succubus fangs, being eaten
alive by some fiend, my nose poking out of hell

seeing double. On one side a filly, the other a gelding,
me with my stubs and you with your long, shapely hands,
the ring on your left still leading me on, your wedding
band, your right, moistened forefinger testing the wind.

Like a sissy, I'd taken to seaweed baths, all the help
I could get, an extra oleaginous film for a skin
too few, long soaks, then dripping in snaky kelp,
trusty trident in hand, I'd rise from my dour domain

to amusement arcades, bars, and dancehalls. Even that gull
in the greying white wedding dress, picking at refuse, ready
to swoop down the aisle again, go for the kill, blushing bridal.
You went back to your hotel, I could see, still hungry.

Your kiss on my cheek, as we parted, officious and tender
enough for me to hang on to see-sawing cliffs,
looking up at the jut of that jaw, then down at the floor,
never taking the measure before for measureless relief,

a steep price to pay, such release, to be beach glass, dull
in and out, for better or worse than divorce, I'd be damned
to repeating that hourglass vow forever, tidal
and true to the fact, each sinner a mere grain of sand

on the strand, where the nuns used to swim, still secluded,
virgin,
after all the invasion, shrewd, uncouth, courting farmers,
stout, dowried daughters of farmers, sealed all but the banns,
holding on to that rope, their one hope, down to the shore.

Never lower, interred in myself like a clam, but I'd married
the sky as a shy altar boy. I could never hide
in a cave wet and fetid with sex. I prayed to the tide
to deliver me home, some dream long ago about suicide.

Transfusion

My heart broke,
not Cupid's cliché,
not even the pulse on the wrist of poetry,
just playing the bones,

the literal,
visceral organ pumping
the stallion, tail and mane ablaze,
round and round our mortal racecourse
at a gallop,

or the sludge,
the trudge of marriage,

or genius
totally blocked by the plaque
of too much language,

thinning into whispers in the theatre,
beeps and pings.
A bell buoy clangs.
A corpse weighed down by stones
sinks further and further, then slips
through a pause in the ocean floor

into this pool
of chlorinated clarity,
medieval certainty,
extremes of horns and haloes
and everything between
delineated, seen,
an oculus cut in the dome,
a quiver of shafts all aimed,

at Abelard
still teaching the sun
the dialectics of the moon,
clinging in a sea of sharks
to the life raft of reason
ripped unexpected
by a vision of the saint within him,
birthing by Caesarian
his Lutgarde.

I could tell by the guttural roughness off my tongue
I was that Flemish nun from Tongres,
my beauty like my dowry squandered,
locked into a convent for safe keeping,
entertaining all and sundry
in the vault of my ignited
body.

Matins, lauds, sext, terce, nones, vespers, compline,
as many canonical hours
as days of the week, seven
uncomprehending, freezing, rote, dying
of boredom, until I found
my tongue, beseeched my spendthrift
Father for the gift of his.

With not so much as a tap
on the bud of my lips
by the tip of his littlest digit
I was zapped literate
in masculine Latin, blooming.
I even assumed the added burden,
the drape and drag, of saying the mass for them.

Understanding everything and feeling nothing,
one morning, sudden as spring,
I had this vision of his son
in the flesh, immaculate and urgent
as the first snowdrop.

And I was impatient as May,
bough bending, lilac heavy,
petulant perfume.

All he had to do was stare at my breasts
to part them, his look a trowel
unearthing my one, unopened bulb
and laying it at my feet, a still birth.

Then the waters of his oceanic chest began to part
and this bounteous, June bouquet,
dripping pink rosé, levitated,
drifted, floated into my sad cavity.
The fit was perfect.
And lest I forget,
before he left, tucked neatly in his pocket,
his one breast
pocket, my dead promise,
where it kicked, although his jacket lay immaculately
flat. Nothing had happened,
just those few, brotherly pats
as he tamped the dirt around that cleft,
adept as a squirrel hiding a nut.

Doves cooed. I took my vows
in a tongue I couldn't taste,
wed a man I couldn't touch,
then crucified him with demands.
Finally, the lance of my lust for everything
got through to him
and he spurted, gushed all over me.

It was wild, whole battlefields of poppies.
bloody cups, vermillion petals, tongues
of flame.

I needed to burn again, sip and suck
a snake bite, taste ambrosial venom,
savour every drop as it clotted
in my mouth, a harvest
of the ripest, darkest, sweetest cherries,
all miraculously free of pits.

North, south, east and west,
breasts and balls, balls and breasts,
a crazed compass
spinning us true north.

Ecstatic, I burst stigmatic.
So, while I sucked at my double,
he/she sucked reciprocally at me,

the mirror of each other, they
were never together alone,

until my narcissistic mystic went
all clinical on me. The house lights up,
the incision in Heaven stitched,
a mask like the first fall of snow
asks with detachment how I am.

Squared

The nuns look after me, leave me free.
They know I'll be back for my tea and brack,
three squares, four walls, my cell in this city
of cloisters. Rounding them keeps me on track.

Fitzwilliam, Merrion, St. Stephen's Green,
Trinity's two quads, then cross the Styx,
Mountjoy, Rutland, Parnell, and between
snaking through Hell, my daily fix.

Common as the clap, she lights a fag,
Bends in a miniskirt, cups her flame.
'What you need,' I mutter, 'is one good shag.'
She fires back a look. Does she know who I am?

I don't, forget, dead for so long down there,
now going upstairs, I live by my tongue,
and pee as the spirit takes me like prayer,
then turn, when I'm lost, to some good Samaritan.

V

Clare

Some might call it balance. At last she sees both sides, caves
below, clouds above, hard fact, vaporous intimations. With
every breath air circulates through one maze, then floats off
into the other. Each day she wakes and chooses to continue
on this surface, desert with the odd oasis.

She's come to rest north of the estuary. First it was seaside,
level as yesterday, then eons, behemoth cliffs, at last the moon,
the plateau of now, the landscape of the end before it dawns, a
spare music. The wind is a *sean nós* singer, a tightrope walker,
toes curled around the thinnest hope, or a lesser animal caught
in the jaws of a greater wailing all the way down.

Here fertility is one, dwarfed orchid on a bed of stone, a
crone having sex in her dreams. An over ripe apple holds on
to a branch, blackberries bleed on the tongue, bread lingers
like the smell of breast milk, lichen precious as jade, fit for
a king, clings to common rock, butterflies are unashamed
of their frivolity (why not?), moths flit because to not gives
the twilight permission to go dark, lips linger on another's
lips, feed off the oozing honey each to each imparts. Two
blossoms kiss. Mouths beat their wings, all soft and sweet
before it's hard and bitter to feel nothing. That's the sting.

Moher

Like measuring light years with a ruler,
inching there at water level
took forever then.

Now, we are the light,
my love and I, riding high,
on the ferry.

In the time it takes a finger to press
send, we roll down
the ramp to the other shore,
delivered,

purr into Killimer,
push on to Kilrush,
wind into Kilkee, in the middle
of July.

Melodeon buttons jumping up and down,
pogoing in the mosh pit,
old typewriter keys in heat.

A carnival on the crab claw strand,
shucked oyster flesh in bathing togs,
donkey rides along the tide line,
winkles in paper, ice cream in wafer
cones, Cadbury stabbed, spiralling
ninety-nines, yesterday without the clouds,
jigging and reeling in the beating sun,
then bidding it all goodbye.

We're on a mission. North.
We take the main route,
the hypotenuse, cutting off
Loop Head.

Doonbeg, Quilty, Milltown Malbay,
flat, flaggy, forlorn shore.
A curlew tests his instrument.
A sandpiper and snipe join in,
the string section
fiddling to find the exact tension
to smooth jagged rock to sand,
a strand with room enough
for everyone to play
even the stocky tern.

We'd stay,
if only there were time, but no.
Lahinch, Liscannor, then on to Moher,
looming like a woolly mammoth.

To drive here is to drive
a wedge into blood-hardened ground.
A barbed arrowhead and polished stone axe
surface iron age grudges,
cashels and bawns,
barrows and middens,
battle and burial in the air,
a trawler in the harbour cemented in silt.
They may have to winch us out.

Circulating through the portaled backbone
of a shrew skeleton this gagging
squeak, pushed, tunnelled through
a plover's elongated beak,
coming out the far end
of the pier as one tin whistle
piping its gleeful keen.

It can be nothing more
than a Sunday ramble,
up the gentle incline to an edge
designed with a T-square,

Frayed feathers waft their warning
down to a base,
as indistinct as memory
of who's alive and dead these days.

We bend our necks as for the guillotine,
and a brutal wind whips up,
an omen of famine,
gusts with the force to shove bright
embers down a chimney's throat,
volcanic waves erupting,
scattering spindrift ash.

Each diaphragm a *bodhrán*,
as Thor pounds
proud cliffs into submission,
brings them to their knees,
all the strata, sagas, wars,
their last breath rubble,

an aftermath of spasms,
generations, the spit
of the dead,
the Hag in the south,
the seed and breed of her marching
north, a petrified parade,
cannon fodder, dust.

Before being up,
has the time to take shape
in the mind, we're down.
Our flock loses heart,
as each pulsing speck breaks
for it, hand in hand
or alone.

Doolin

If this is hell, then thank you, Charon.
I might have known you'd be here,
invisible in your loincloth, listening
to the music of the spheres,

a measured orgy, stone on the edge
of ocean, a buoyant *seisiún*,
mad clapping and tapping, extremities only,
you sipping on nothing but Lethean

sound, while standing at attention
like that step dancer soldier numb
from the knees on up, his way to stay level-
headed in case of mayhem.

Caves under parchment skin, flayed karst
ahead, the unsaid. What keeps
this room glued together, away from the cliffs
is trusting how each note leaps

at the chance to dance with or defend
another against the fear
of all the fiddles gone, the whistle going
where it's never been before,

a pitch black place, the jolly melodeon
on Prozac. Then, it's all diddly di
play again. Each one has the other's back,
a bit of auld *craic*. Family.

As you come up for air, we go under
to smell a grieved perfume,
see in the dark, even hear in the coffin
the rhythm of that drum.

Stay with us Charon. The march of that wind.
In Doolin we swam in oblivion.
We'd skipped the Acheron, river of pain.
Now we're in for it in the Burren.

Longboat

The nave out of kilter, a skewed chancel arch,
consoling, homey details.
We screw up, wind down, try to patch
it up, chip at the ideal.

But people wobble. Take that foundation.
Were they distracted? Drunk?
Or lost in translation, a French stonemason
ordering Irish monks?

Did the abbot look down his long, Cistercian
nose at that scentless muguet
drilled in rock, as alien on this barren
surface as he. Pure folly,

not knowing invasion has its benefits.
Granted, Saint Bernard's boys,
he'd admit, like playing with half-men, illicit
centaurs, the order's toys.

But that takes balls, not this weak predilection
for adolescent dragons,
meek flowers, the spread legs of frigid chevrons,
no hunter winding his horn.

Flagrance and prudence, famine and plague,
like putting the wind on hold,
They needed that lily, the medic's exotic,
a cardiac tonic, gold,

still is. The calm of Corcomroe is real
as a flight of fancy. Some artisan
sketched a longboat in lime on the wall.
It still rides the waves of stone.

So transported, I can see us living here.
An abbot and abbess? No.
A common nun and a local farmer
teaching her all he knows

about how to grow an apple, sweet and tart.
I'm footing his forked, wooden ladder
looking up the length of his keel, and my heart
veers into dangerous water

so calm, and safety, he knows, makes me wild,
riding his gentle ripples.
I retreat to the kitchen, my sisters. My smile
is an itch I can't scratch. It tickles.

My raison d'être had been a mess,
Aberlard's, my Paraclete.
He could holy ghost a whole forest to ash.
Then, I'd clean out the grate.

Now tongues of flesh whisper their bliss,
Genesis lighting the dark,
the muscular prayer of a French kiss
to Our Lady of the Fertile Rock.

Practice

'Begin,' says the dawn, then complicates it,
'by finding your meditation posture,
comfortable yet upright.'
But which end's up?

With clouds below and caves above,
the Burren in between,
a dot, a train of thought,
her 'present time awareness,'

karst is a two-way mirror.
Stone sky weighs hard on the air
we walk on, cracks a window
onto God-knows-where reflected.

Boston to Shannon descending
sleepless on the edge of morning,
beneath us the lumpy mattress
Goliath left for the tide to recycle.

Cruising at an altitude,
our airbus dozed on a featherbed,
plummeted, panicked, turbulence
smoothed by another faceless voice.

The blind read a map tap by tap.
With every tentative step I pound
a drum, head in the clouds,
trip on a knuckle of actual rock,

rip through flesh thinner than air,
snake through cumulus caverns,
calciferous rivers, grykes
on a tongue long extinct,

until she speaks, that dis-embodied
voice, inviting me, 'to sink
into the body, investigate
the body,' she stresses, her emphasis

on torture, 'clench the jaw in your gut,'
make Cerberus give up,
give back your breath,
'You always have your breath,'

she reassures. Her 'always'
makes me anxious. It's big and I'm small,
a snail, a cave, a nostril, a mortal
length of dry stone wall,

flying up and over the skull of Moneen,
the scar from an axe murder,
diagram of the brain,
left and right, tuition, intuition,

haphazard and planned,
as a river makes decisions,
each herringbone and crenellation
a knitting pattern handed down.

In the end, it takes a matchmaker
to assess the 'posture, shape, and weight,'
most, the innate friction
of every slab. Will it mate? Stick

to another, yet let air circulate,
minimal material (we all get tired)
for maximum endurance. A wall
of resistance is bound to fall.

Sheep startle, when they face
a fact and get a hole, a fishing net
netting the light, aphasia
hooking the word by forgetting to fret.

Just sit there and submit
to the wind, the odd fix, a hip, a knee,
play snakes and ladders, if needs be,
with fossil tubes and spirals,

be spooked by spiders, egged on by cuckoos,
study the life style of lichens,
tar balancing snow, mustard
to zip up your too steady diet

of algae, moss and ferns, all heavy
on anti-oxidants, perfect fare
for ponderous rats and stoats,
the requisite fox, old goat, the bollox,

but I stray. That's ok, says she,
who anticipates my sins.
Fidget like a pipit, swing like Tarzan
through the canopy, so long as you

return to the breath. I'm trying
to get good at it, to stand
on my head in time. Instead, I sit
with the din of now,

until it too needs vital quiet
killed by a little bell. Waves fade
like breaths. I get up, stretch,
begin the day that's in it. Zazen.

Lips

I'm a hag, mad and frank, Medusa turned to stone,
Free to speak hard words, put shape on what was molten.

My mother floats in ocean. Boobs bob, legs spread
Like a Sheela na gig. Spiders. Touch yours and you're dead.

The rod of the serpent banished mine, one tongue flick,
Nothing, a tickle, a kick, and then harpoon ripped,

Up the middle like a whale. My shell eyes spiralled,
As Hell gave birth to Heaven, those lips on my nipple.

Under the lash flesh petrifies, I'd long been frozen,
Then opened my mouth in the Arctic and spoke ice floes.

Limestone acts as a storage radiator. The glacier
Smoulders, a flick of the switch and residual pleasure,

Seeing my grandmother. No breasts. No womb. Bitter
Loss, but she was like grass growing all the sweeter

Forced up through a crack, her eye on the light. Here calves
Suckle on honeyed udders, grow fat on love.

And the local Sheela na gig each spring with the gentians
Lactates, warm milk from stone dugs at the thought of her
son.

Portal

Precious oblations, stone beads, a pendant, a stillborn,
a doll's inarticulate bones, the cairn in the tomb,
in its pit, young and old, facing north, at Poulnabrone.

The roof of that mouth, a slab weighing tons, is charm
speaking horror, a balancing act, so long as the portal
holds. She too needs a trinket to ward off more harm.

An arrowhead wedged in a hip. This flesh was special,
exposed first to air, then vultures, then fire, aristocracy
purged, pecked carrion clean, bone scorched immortal.

More and more, I study the lightsome ways of butterflies,
the grayling adjusting its gnomon to cast no shadow,
the wood white with wings of deathly pallor, seen only

when crushed, a ghost on the ghost of a wall. Poor Plato,
tongues of light in his cave, echoes, the shadows all flown.
Another cadaver to consume, another ego.

In the high Burren, now, on the plateau up near Carron,
A wave moth flits its forgiveness on all that bone.

VI

The Word

A three-way mirror

Judgment

Harpoon riled as Leviathan, I dove lower
Than any sea monster ever. Not half far enough.
I came back from Tír na nÓg both old and sober,

Knowing the hawk of justice is no flitting moth.
My body's a timber ship, gold bullion my soul.
Too soon from the crow's nest, the edge of this world hoves.

Is he in Hell, I ask, who rendered all touch foul?
He brushed some hair out of my eyes. It burned.
That smudge turned to ash, to soot inside my cowl.

I took my vows. Now, I'm judged for sins of omission,
Not those I chose to resist, to protect above
All others, my flesh resurrected, my self, my son,

To whom I've shown nothing, as I was shown, but love.

Finis